# YOUR KNOWLEDGE HAS VALUE

- We will publish your bachelor's and master's thesis, essays and papers

- Your own eBook and book - sold worldwide in all relevant shops

- Earn money with each sale

Upload your text at www.GRIN.com
and publish for free

**Bibliographic information published by the German National Library:**

The German National Library lists this publication in the National Bibliography; detailed bibliographic data are available on the Internet at http://dnb.dnb.de .

This book is copyright material and must not be copied, reproduced, transferred, distributed, leased, licensed or publicly performed or used in any way except as specifically permitted in writing by the publishers, as allowed under the terms and conditions under which it was purchased or as strictly permitted by applicable copyright law. Any unauthorized distribution or use of this text may be a direct infringement of the author s and publisher s rights and those responsible may be liable in law accordingly.

**Imprint:**

Copyright © 2017 GRIN Verlag
Print and binding: Books on Demand GmbH, Norderstedt Germany
ISBN: 9783668717343

**This book at GRIN:**

https://www.grin.com/document/427722

Leon Gregori

# International Business Communication. Case Study Research based on theories of Hofstede and Hall

GRIN Verlag

**GRIN - Your knowledge has value**

Since its foundation in 1998, GRIN has specialized in publishing academic texts by students, college teachers and other academics as e-book and printed book. The website www.grin.com is an ideal platform for presenting term papers, final papers, scientific essays, dissertations and specialist books.

**Visit us on the internet:**

http://www.grin.com/

http://www.facebook.com/grincom

http://www.twitter.com/grin_com

California State University, Sacramento
AKAD University, Stuttgart

**CSUS Pre-Arrival Assignment 2017**
**Intercultural Competence**

Created by:     Leon Gregori
Deadline:       08.10.2017
Submit Date:    22.09.2017

**Table of contents**

1. Incident One, German presentation to Americans .................... 3
   1.1 Root Cause .................... 3
   1.2 Root Cause Analysis .................... 3
2. Incident Two, Business Meeting in Mexico City .................... 4
   2.1 Root Cause .................... 4
   2.2 Root Cause Analysis .................... 5
   2.3 Evaluation of other answers .................... 6
3. Incident Three, Interview in Shanghai .................... 6
   3.1 Root Cause .................... 7
   3.2 Root Cause Analysis .................... 7
4. Bibliography .................... 8

**Table of figures**

Figure 1: Mr. Bauer versus US Engineers: Hofstede's dimensions .................... 4
Figure 2: Mr. Meier versus Mr. Perez: Hofstede's dimensions .................... 6
Figure 3: High- and low-context cultures .................... 7

# 1. Incident One, German presentation to Americans

## 1.1 Root Cause

The best answer to justify the behavior of the American engineers during the business meeting with the German department manager (Gerhardt Bauer) is that "Gerhardt's prognosis that the North American market would stagnate was not well taken by the American audience."[1]

## 1.2 Root Cause Analysis

Mr. Bauer's task is to represent his company as well as to present interesting opportunities for the medical engineers, who want to evaluate a possible joint-venture. By stating out that "the North America market will become less important in the years to come, due to saturation of the market"[2] Mr. Bauer does not promote his products very well, thus the engineers are not interested in his presentation. Although it is not clear if the Americans are interested in the North American market or other global markets, they could become upset as either Mr. Bauer's product is not good enough to hit the American market or the American market has no buying power and a weak economy. As we know, Mr. Bauer as a German is long-term oriented (See also figure 1) and does not see possibilities in the North American market. That is why it is possible that the Americans evaluated the North American market more on a short-term base, which assumes profitability until the market saturation sets in.

If Mr. Bauer had been more optimistic, the engineers would have been much more attentive, "presentations should not only be relevant and well researched but also delivered in a positive, enthusiastic and committed manner."[3] Analyzing the other possible answers, answer "b" is also a valid option as "Communications should be timely, unless the objective of a communication is

---

[1] LÜNEMANN, Ulrich. Intercultural Competence. CSUS Pre-Arrival Assignment 2017, Page 2
[2] LÜNEMANN, Ulrich. Intercultural Competence. CSUS Pre-Arrival Assignment 2017, Page 2
[3] WARBURTON, Keith. American Meetings, Global Business Culture

to transfer historical information or information that is not time-sensitive"[4] and indeed, the engineers are not so much interested in the historical information Mr. Bauer provided. But still this should not be a reason to be disrespectful and start talking during a business presentation. Answer "c" has also a point of truth as the engineers seem to have the requirement to communicate during the business meeting. Instead of having an exchange of ideas or a dialogue with Mr. Bauer, they just discourse unprofessionally within the audience instead of discussing directly with the presenter.

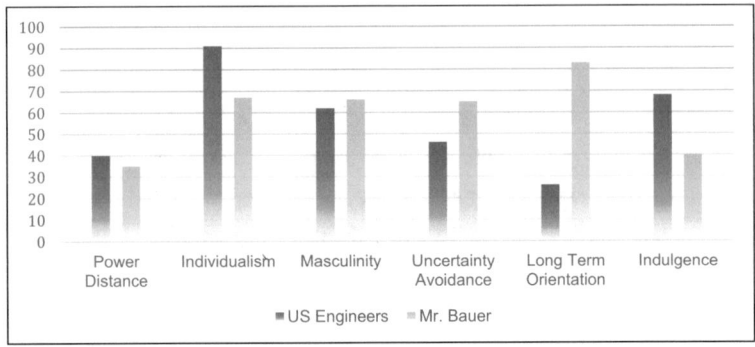

Figure 1: Mr. Bauer versus US Engineers: Hofstede's dimensions[5], own representation

## 2. Incident Two, Business Meeting in Mexico City

### 2.1 Root Cause

The main underlying issue between Mr. Meier and Mr. Perez is the difference in their cultural values. While Mr. Meier is always focused on doing business related negotiation, Mr. Perez as well as his colleagues are anxious about building a personal relationship with Mr. Meier. The issue or moreover misunderstanding agitates in the differences of the German and Mexican communication culture:

---

[4] YARDLEY, David. Practical Consultancy Ethics: Professional Excellence for IT and Management Consultants, Kogan Page Publishers, 2017, Chapter 7, Page 4
[5] HOFSTEDE, Geert; BOND, Michael H. Hofstede's culture dimensions, Page 417-433

"Germans are not used to build personal relationship with their business partners. It is a common practice to clearly distinguish private life and business activities."[6]. This does not match with the character of Mexican communication culture which is far more personal:
"For Mexicans, building a personal relationship with the partner is important. It gives them the feeling they can trust their partner."[7]
As Mr. Meier is interested in getting the contract signed[8] he should have paid more attention to the cultural differences between Germans and Mexicans, to avoid struggling in his presentation.

2.2 Root Cause Analysis

As ""Leveraging relationships is an important element when negotiating in Mexico"[9] the best answer of the provided possibilities is that "Mr. Perez is genuinely trying to develop a relationship of trust with Peter Meier so that he can reach an agreement quickly when it comes to the negotiation."[10] Further shown in the below comparison of Hofstede's cultural dimensions (figure 2), Indulgence and Individualism are spread widely between Mr. Perez and Mr. Meier, resulting in different communication structure and business negotiation alike. Mexicans live the collectivism, where especially relationship building and networking are important to become successful. In comparison, the German culture is more individualistic and result oriented.

---

[6] ROJANAWISUT, Bastien; XIONG LO, Chu; et al. "Business between Germany and Mexico" Page. 19
[7] ROJANAWISUT, Bastien; XOING LO, Chu; et al. "Business between Germany and Mexico" Page. 18
[8] cf. LÜNEMANN, Ulrich. Intercultural Competence. CSUS Pre-Arrival Assignment 2017, Page 3
[9] KATZ, Lothar. Negotiating international business, Page 4.
[10] LÜNEMANN, Ulrich. Intercultural Competence. CSUS Pre-Arrival Assignment 2017, Page 3

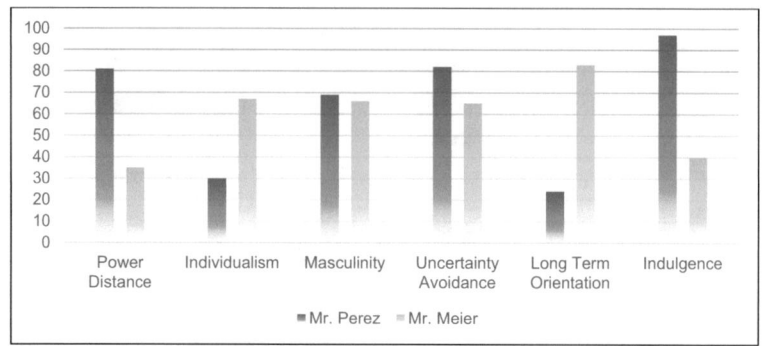

Figure 2: Mr. Meier versus Mr. Perez: Hofstedes dimensions[11], own representation

2.3 Evaluation of other answers

Answer D is already stated out in section 3.2, Answer A, B and C are all somehow valid due to "Negotiators in the country may use pressure techniques that include making final offers, applying time pressure, showing intransigence, or nibbling."[12]. Furthermore, it is very normal that negotiations in Mexico take time. "Expect negotiations to be slow and protracted. Be prepared to make several trips if necessary to achieve your objectives. Relationship building, information gathering, bargaining, and decision making may take considerable time. Attempts to rush the process are unlikely to produce better results and may be viewed as offensive. Throughout the negotiation, participants need to be patient, control their emotions, and accept the inevitable delays."[13]. As the duration of negotiations is wordy by default and not only because Mr. Perez and his managers want more time and finally considering the core value of personal relationships, Answer D is the most realistic.

# 3. Incident Three, Interview in Shanghai

---

[11] HOFSTEDE, Geert; BOND, Michael H. Hofstede's culture dimensions, Page 417-433
[12] KATZ, Lothar. Negotiating international business, Page 5.
[13] KATZ, Lothar. Negotiating international business, Page 4.

## 3.1 Root Cause

Essential for the challenge between Karin and the Chinese recruiters is the Chinese high context culture which is not understood by Karin; "Since the companies did not want to embarrass Karin and make her "loose face," they tried to relay their message through nonverbal cues such as delaying the answer and simply not replying"[14]

## 3.2 Root Cause Analysis

German people in general and in this specific case Karin need to build up a relationship first to correctly understand the context of the conversation or communication with the Chinese interviewers. For Karin, knowing only the German low context culture, everything unspoken is considered as unknown, thus during communication everyone tries to be as precise as possible to have a clear common understanding. This common understanding is missing as the Chinese high context culture does not foresee the precise German communication and therefore no response or feedback is given to a job applicant in case of a non-successful interview. As this is very common for Chinese culture, the other answers offered are not that valid considering the high context culture where there is no option that the Chinese Interviewers want to be rude or are against foreigners. This is just how the communication works and Karin was not aware.

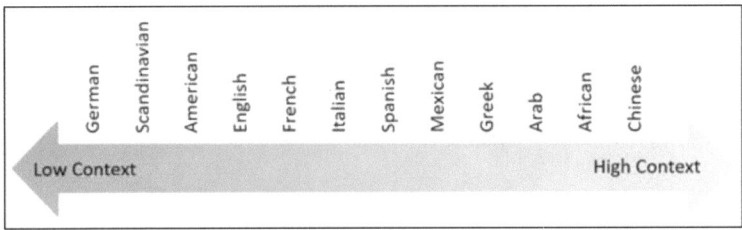

Figure 3: High- and low-context cultures[15], own representation

---

[14] LÜNEMANN, Ulrich. Intercultural Competence. CSUS Pre-Arrival Assignment 2017, Page 5
[15] NEESE, Brian, Intercultural Communication. High- and Low-Context cultures, 2016

## 4. Bibliography

HOFSTEDE, Geert; BOND, Michael H. Hofstede's culture dimensions: An independent validation using Rokeach's value survey. Journal of cross-cultural psychology, 1984

KATZ, Lothar. Negotiating international business: The negotiator's reference guide to 50 countries around the world. Createspace Independent Pub, 2006

LÜNEMANN, Ulrich. Intercultural Competence. CSUS Pre-Arrival Assignment 2017, 2017

NEESE, Brian, Intercultural Communication. High- and Low-Context cultures, 2016
(21.09.2017)
http://online.seu.edu/high-and-low-context-cultures/

Rojanawisut, Bastien, Xiong Lo, Chu et al. "Business between Germany and Mexico: Cultural Analysis and Comparison from a Business Perspective." (2010) S. 19
(21.09.2017)
https://www.iei.liu.se/indek/utbildning/industriell-marknadsforing/teim03/file-archive-2015/1.658320/group5_GermanyVsLatinAmerica.pdf

WARBURTON, Keith. American Meetings, Global Business Culture,
(21.09.2017)
www.worldbusinessculture.com

YARDLEY, David. Practical Consultancy Ethics: Professional Excellence for IT and Management Consultants, Kogan Page Publishers, 2017

# YOUR KNOWLEDGE HAS VALUE

- We will publish your bachelor's and master's thesis, essays and papers

- Your own eBook and book - sold worldwide in all relevant shops

- Earn money with each sale

Upload your text at www.GRIN.com
and publish for free